What happened next?

Redvers Brandling

Edward Arnold

Preface

Do you like solving mysteries? Are you good at spotting clues in written pieces of evidence? Do you ever wonder 'what happened next' when you have got *nearly* all the facts about something?

In the pages which follow you will read some files about many things – a message in a bottle; an advertisement for a space cadet; the sighting of a UFO; an aeroplane with its passengers travelling outside(!); the story of how two letters got mixed up; opinions about a comedian; the story of a competition, and several others.

When you have read these files you will be asked if you can 'spot clues' which they all contain, and which will help you to use your imagination in solving mysteries and deciding what happened next.

When you have finished this book you might like to make up some files of your own – and test your friends with them.

Good luck!

First published 1985
by Edward Arnold (Publishers) Ltd
41 Bedford Square
London WC1B 3DQ

Edward Arnold (Australia) Pty Ltd
80 Waverley Road
Caulfield East
Victoria 3145
Australia

British Library Cataloguing in Publication Data

Brandling, Redvers
What happened next?
1. English language—Examinations, questions, etc.
I. Title
428.2 PE1112

ISBN 0–7131–7450–1

Contents

Acknowledgements

The Publishers would like to thank the following for permission to reproduce copyright material:

Findlay Publications for a chart from *Geriatric Medicine* April 1982; *The Royal Life Saving Society – U.K.* for material from their 'Blue Code' for Water Safety on pages 8 and 9; *The London Express News and Feature Services* for the photograph on page 44 and Steve Richards for the photograph on page 28.

Designed and typeset in 11/13 Melior by DP Press, Sevenoaks, Kent
Printed in Great Britain by The Bath Press, Avon

1 Points of view

ROVERS TO MOVE OUT OF TOWN

Mr. Team

Mr. Ivor Team, Chairman of Bootley Rovers, announced that next year the team will be playing at a new stadium. 'A successful First Division team like us needs a ground which will hold 50,000 people – and has car parks to match. We've found just the place for this. It's a village called Steeple Lonely, 3 miles from Bootley. There's plenty of room to build a big ground with all the facilities we need there.'

Plan of the Development

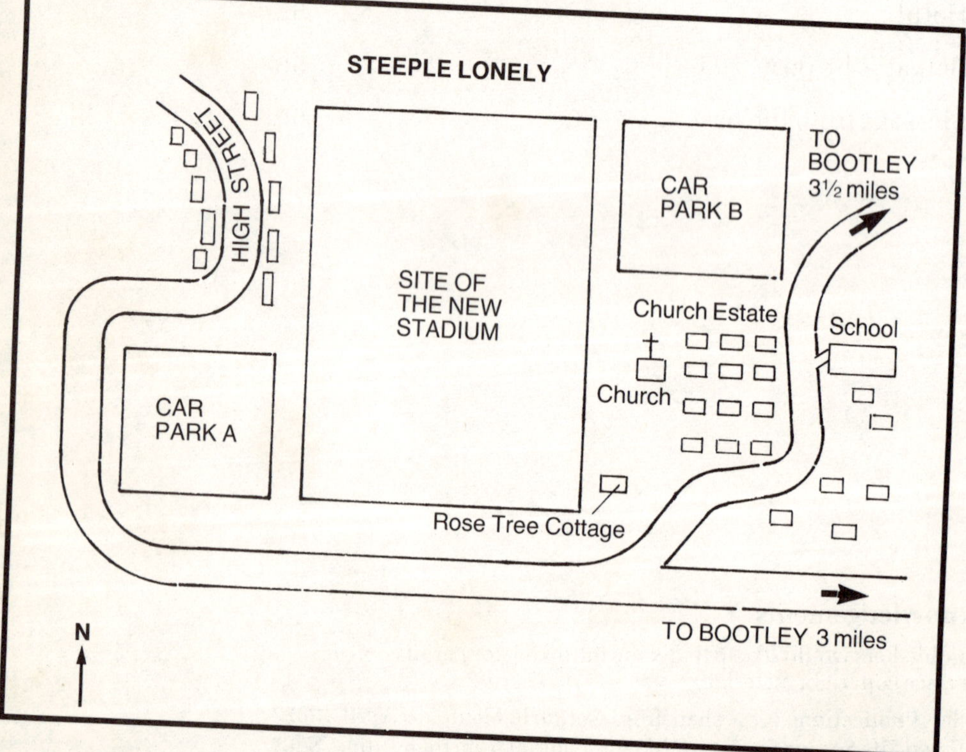

Bootley Echo 23/9/93

Roker Road,
Bootley.
25/3/93.

Mr. I. Team,
Bootley Rovers,
Bootley.

Dear Mr. Team, Please, please don't move Rovers out to Steeple Lonely!
My friends and I are all 12 and we are all Rovers fans. We walk to the ground now – but it would be very difficult for us to get to Steeple Lonely. Think of your real fans!

Yours imploringly, Sep Porter.

"SAW YOUR ANNOUNCEMENT IN THE PRESS IVOR. O.K., THE DEAL IS ON. WE'LL GIVE YOU £400,000 FOR THE STADIUM IN BOOTLEY. WE'LL KNOCK IT DOWN AND THEN BUILD 200 HOUSES ON IT. THAT WAY WE'LL BOTH MAKE A PROFIT!"

Miss Theresa Green – lives in Rose Tree Cottage, Steeple Lonely. She loves gardening and has many roses. She likes the countryside and hates towns and noise. She has 6 cats.

Sid Floggit – owns a sweets/cigarettes/drinks/papers shop in Steeple Lonely High Street. He has never made much profit because there aren't many customers.

Mrs. Jackie Pimot – has two children. Her husband works in Bootley. They would like to own a house in Bootley but can't find one. They hear rumours that houses are going to be built on site of present football ground.

1 Points of view

When you have read carefully all the pieces of information about **Points of view**, do the following:

A

Answer the following questions in sentences.

1 In which division do Bootley Rovers play?
2 Give two reasons why the Chairman says the team should move to Steeple Lonely.
3 Which of the car parks is east of the stadium?
4 Why do you think it will be more difficult for Sep Porter to get to the new ground than the present one?
5 Do you think a car-owning fan would feel the same as Sep? Give a reason for your answer.
6 Who do you think is one person Mr Team might be helping if the present stadium is knocked down and houses built where it stands now?
7 How many roads lead from Steeple Lonely to Bootley?
8 Do you think Rovers' new ground will hold more, or less, people than their present one? Give a reason for your answer.
9 Do you think Steeple Lonely school will be a large or small one?
10 Do you think fans coming from Bootley would be likely to pass Rose Tree Cottage on their way to the new ground?

B

Bearing in mind what you know from reading all the pieces, do the following:

1 Write a letter from Miss Green to a friend, saying what she thinks about this idea of building a football stadium in Steeple Lonely.
2 Look at the small picture of Mr Team. Draw a full length picture of how you imagine he would look.
3 Imagine you are Mrs Jackie Pimot and write a letter to the editor of the *Bootley Echo* saying why you think Rovers should move.

C

Write down what you think each of the following words means. Check with a dictionary to see if your definitions are correct.

announced **facilities** **profit** **rumours** **site**

D

Re-write the following paragraph. Fill in the blanks with what you think are suitable words. Check with the 'facts' when you need to.

> Perhaps Mr Team really does think Rovers will be better off at Steeple Lonely, but he is also interested in making some ____ for himself. The two people we know who least want Rovers to move are ____ ____ and ____ ____. Although they both want Rovers to stay in Bootley their reasons for wanting this are not the ____. Sid ____'s shop is situated in ____ Street, Steeple Lonely. This is on the ____ side of the new stadium.

E

Choose one of the following and with a friend, or friends, prepare either a short mime or play about it.

1 People sometimes give a reason for wanting something – which is not their *real* reason. Imagine that Sid Floggit meets Ivor Team. Think about what he might say about Mr Team's 'great idea' of moving Rovers. Then think what he might say to his wife that night when he gives the real reasons he wants Rovers to move to Steeple Lonely.

2 Can you make up more of the conversation between the mystery telephone caller and Ivor Team?

3 **Use your imagination** – Miss Green decides on a protest when the builders start arriving to put up the new stadium. What does she say, write and do? What do the newspapers/TV do? What happens? What are the consequences?

F

1 From what you *know* about the facts, write out a 'character study' of Ivor Team. Be as detailed as you can.

2 Invent another character who does *not* want Rovers to leave Bootley. Work out some reasons why this is the case. They could live in either Bootley or Steeple Lonely.

2 The accident

16th July

Dear Jack,

Listen to this good news. My folks are letting me go on holiday with just Jason Black next week! We're going to stay with his brother at Minton-on-sea – right on the beach!

Mum has been going on a bit – has even given me a copy of the Blue Code for Water Safety – me, with a Bronze Medal!

I can't wait to go! I'll tell you all about it when I get back.

Thats all for now. Billy

THE BLUE CODE FOR WATER SAFETY

1 DON'T GO ALONE

Whether swimming, boating or even fishing, *don't go alone. Water safety starts on land and this leaflet tells you how.*

2 IF YOU FALL IN AND CAN'T REACH SAFETY, FLOAT ON YOUR BACK

a. Try to stay calm.
b. Turn over and float on your back.
c. Attract attention by waving *one* arm and shouting for help.

3 IF SOMEONE ELSE FALLS IN DON'T GO IN THE WATER AFTER HIM

a. Don't panic.
b. Look for something to help pull him out – stick, rope or clothing.
c. Lie down to prevent yourself from being pulled in.
d. If you cannot reach him, throw any floating object – football, plastic bottle – for him to hold on to, *then fetch help.*

THE 999 DRILL

You do *not* need coins to make an emergency call. The operator will answer a 999 call and ask:-

1. Which service you require.

2. Your telephone number.

You ask for the ***Police*** (or the ***Coastguard*** if near the coast). The Police or Coastguard will then ask you:-

1. What the trouble is.

2. Where it is.

3. Whether anyone is capable of taking action while help is arriving.

4. The telephone number you are speaking from.

5. Your name and address.

By knowing what the questions will be and being able to answer them you will speed the arrival of the emergency services.

Surfing Black and white flags mark areas for surfing. It is unwise to bathe in these areas.

THE KISS OF LIFE

How to do it

1. Lift the jaw and tilt the head back again.

2. Keep the casualty's mouth closed, seal your mouth over his nose and give four quick breaths. Watch for his chest to rise, this will show you are getting air into his lungs.

3. Raise your head to allow the casualty to breathe out (the chest will fall).

4. Repeat the sequence with one blow every 5 seconds. Keep the Kiss of Life going until breathing starts again. This may be a very long time but don't stop until a Doctor or the ambulance arrives.

5. If the mouth to nose method does not make the chest rise try the method of mouth to mouth.

a) Pinch the nose shut.

b) Keep the head tilted.

c) Keep the chin lifted.

d) Seal your mouth over the casualty's and breathe the same as for mouth to nose.

MINTON-ON-SEA

ECHO

SISTERS SAVE SWIMMER

Billy Cairns, aged 14, is in hospital recovering from a swimming accident on Boogie Board Beach. This took place last Saturday, 25th July, when Cairns, ignoring a surfing flag, got into difficulties in rough water.

He was saved by the quick thinking of Jenny and Vicki Carini, aged 13. Jenny gave him the kiss of life on the beach, Vicki called 999.

Billy said, "I was really stupid. I owe my life to those two girls and I am very grateful!"

2 The accident

When you have read carefully all the pieces of information about **The accident**, do the following:

A

Answer the following questions in sentences.

1 How many people were going with Billy to Minton-on-Sea?
2 What is the surname of the person with whom Billy and Jason are going to stay?
3 What do you think Billy has a bronze medallion for?
4 Why does *The Blue Code* say you should not go swimming alone?
5 What is the best position to be in, on land, if you are trying to pull somebody out of the water?
6 What sort of flag do you think was flying on Boogie Board Beach on 25th July?
7 How much money do you need to make a 999 call?
8 What exactly do you think 'got into difficulties' means in the *Echo* report?
9 Why was it good that two people arrived to help Billy?
10 What do you think was stupid about Billy's actions?

B

Bearing in mind what you know from reading all the pieces, do the following:

1 Use your imagination and write down the reasons why Jason Black was not with Billy on Saturday, 25th July.
2 Describe exactly what you think happened between Billy going for a swim on Boogie Board Beach – and finishing up in hospital.
3 What qualities do you think a beach life-guard needs to have?

C

Write down what you think each of the following words means. Check with a dictionary to see if your definitions are correct.

attention **surfing** **emergency** **casualty** **sequence**

D

Re-write the following paragraph. Fill in the blanks with what you think are suitable words. Check with the 'facts' when you need to.

Billy Cairns thought his mother was being fussy when she gave him a ____ of *The Blue Code*. Because he had a ____ he thought he would never get into ____ when he was swimming. He behaved very ____ when he ignored the surfing flag on the beach and he was lucky that ____ Carini saved him with the ____ of life. When Billy was in ____ he realised how foolish he had been.

E

Choose one of the following and with a friend, or friends, prepare either a short mime or play about it.

1 How Mrs Cairns found out about Billy's accident.
2 The scene at Boogie Board Beach when the Carini sisters saw what had happened to Billy.
3 What happened when Vicki's 999 call was received.

F

1 Perhaps when Billy finally got home again his mother would write to the Carini twins thanking them for their help. Think about what she might say and then write 'her' letter.
2 Young people often do foolish things because of 'dares'. Work out a story in which this is the reason behind Billy's accident. What is the dare? Who suggests it? What happened about it?
3 Imagine that, because of his experiences, Billy is asked to give a talk to a Bronze Medallion swimming class. Work out a talk of about two minutes, pretend you are Billy, give it to the class.

3 Letter to George

1 Gladrag Way,
Oakingham,
Boakshire,
5th May.

Hi George!
Heard you were back in town – so get this!
We're going to swing in the grounds of "The Grange" on 29th June – a fab disco.
See you there – save a dance for me.
Love,
Wanda.

Lord George Plum-Chokely,
"The Grange,"
Oakley,
Boakshire.

1 Gladrag Way,
Oakingham,
Boakshire,
5th May.

Dear Lord George,

We would be grateful for your permission to hold a disco in the grounds of The Grange on 29th June.

We would, of course, pay whatever charges are necessary and would make absolutely sure that there was no damage or inconvenience caused.

Our committee would be pleased to meet you at your convenience to discuss arrangements.

Yours sincerely

Wanda Rock

Secretary,
Oakingham Youth Groups

First Class

George Plumley,
21 Gumple Street,
Oakingham,
Boakshire.

Lord George Plum-Chokely,
"The Grange,"
Oakley,
Boakshire.

Lord George Plum-Chokeley

60 years old; owns a large factory; likes hunting and shooting; has just returned to England after a business trip; has a 'haughty' wife; always appears very prim and proper BUT secretly he loves pop music and discos.

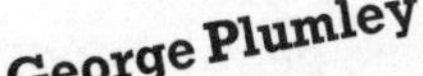

George Plumley

17 years old; very popular with all age groups; a great practical joker; expects people to play jokes on him and is always trying them on other people; his favourite hobby is dancing at which he is very good.

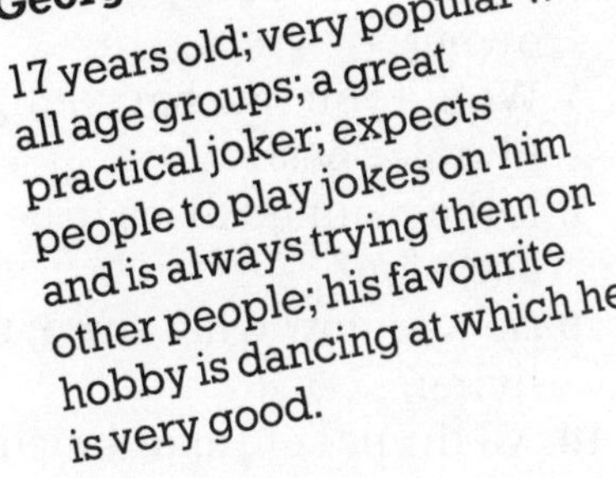

Lady Plum-Chokeley

59-year-old wife of Lord George; does not like many people – particularly if they are young; hates pop music BUT knows and likes George Plumley and thinks he is wonderful because he once saved her poodle from being run over.

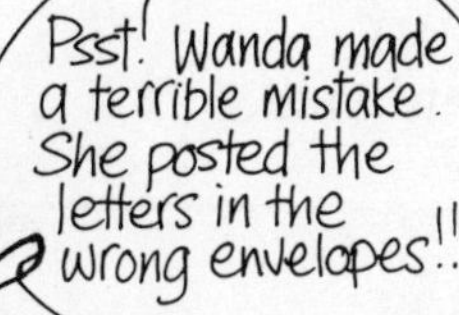

When you have read carefully all the pieces of information about **Letter to George**, do the following:

A

Answer the following questions in sentences.

1 What position with the Oakingham Youth Groups does Wanda Rock hold?
2 Do you think Wanda Rock has ever met George Plumley before?
3 Why does Wanda think George Plumley will want to dance at the disco?
4 What is Lord George's secret?
5 What do you think George Plumley thought when he got the 'wrong' letter?
6 Which of the people mentioned do we know to be a pet owner?
7 Would you say that young or old people liked George Plumley best?
8 Is the planned disco to be an indoor or outdoor occasion?
9 Do we know what any of the mentioned people do for a living?
10 All the people mentioned have one thing in common. What is it?

B

Bearing in mind what you know from reading all these pieces, do the following:

1 **Use your imagination** – describe how Wanda finds out about the mistake she has made.
2 Imagine you are George Plumley and write a letter back to Wanda. Remember you are a great joker!
3 What 'arrangements' do you think are needed when a disco has to be organised?

C

Write down what you think each of the following words means. Check with a dictionary to see if your definitions are correct.

grateful **permission** **inconvenience**
haughty **practical-joker**

D

Re-write the following paragraph. Fill in the blanks with what you think are suitable words. Check with the 'facts' when you need to.

We know that Wanda has made a terrible ____ by putting the letters in the wrong ____ . George Plumley probably thinks that the letter he has got is some sort of ____ . Lord George however might be angry at getting a letter telling him there is going to be a disco in his own ____ ! When we know more about the people we realise that some very interesting things would happen on the night of the ____ .

E

Choose one of the following and with a friend, or friends, prepare either a short mime or play about it.

1 How Lord George and his wife acted when they got Wanda's letter – what they said, what they did, and what they said they would do.
2 How Wanda found out about her mistake and what she did about it.
3 Work out a slightly longer play about what happens on the night of the disco – bearing in mind the 'secrets' you know about each of the people.

F

1 Imagine that Lord George does not realise he has got the wrong letter. Is he annoyed or pleased or flattered by Wanda's letter? Make up your own mind and then, imagining you are Lord George, write a letter back to Wanda.
2 'How a poodle saved the night.' Using your imagination, and remembering the link between Lady Plum-Chokeley and George Plumley, write an exciting/amusing story about the night of the disco using the title given here.
3 If George Plumley thought the letter he got was a practical joke he might decide to play one back on Wanda. What might it be? Look again at Wanda's letter to Lord George before you decide.

4 What's your advice?

Sue Tibble,
'Problem Page',
'Daily Recorder',
London WC2

10 Gable Street,
Thorney Hill,
Co. Durham.

20th June.

Dear Sue Tibble,

Can you help me? My parents are very worried about my Gran who is 75 years old. She lives by herself, doesn't keep her flat warm enough and seems to have lost interest in everything.

In a month's time it is her birthday and my mum would like to buy her something which would really make her take an interest in life again. Have you any suggestions? I hope you can help.

Yours sincerely,

Saloni Garascar.

The following chart shows why people value pets. The scores are marked on the scale which shows **1** as the most important and **9** as the least important.

Age	16–25	25–65	65 and over
Makes me feel safe	5	8	3
Helps make friends	7	4	5
Gives you something to talk about	3	4	7
Its activities are interesting	7	1	6
Gives you something to do	9	7	8
Something to talk to	5	9	5
Helps keep you active	3	1	3
Provides 24 hour companionship	2	4	1
Something to care for	1	3	2

Walter
Rather bad tempered cat; refuses to be kept in; often suffers minor injuries in fights; often scratches furniture.

Oscar
A large mongrel; needs lots of room and exercise; good for protection; does not like to stay in one place for very long; a very strong dog.

Favourite pets in Great Britain in 1981:–

5.7 million dogs;
5.2 million cats;
1.9 million budgies.

"... a doctor recently told this paper that many old people cared more about their pets than themselves – and this helped them! For instance an old lady might be tempted to save on heating for herself – but not if her bird was uncomfortable ..."

FACT FILE

Mrs Aliya Gavascar

Age: 75

Home: 1 bedroomed, fourth floor flat in tower block.

Health: good but cannot move fast or walk very far.

Interests: very few since her husband died; always enjoyed 'looking after' a family; keeps flat very neat and tidy. Lonely at the moment.

Sue Tibble,
"Problem Page",
1st July

Dear Saloni,

Thanks for your letter about the problem concerning your Gran. I think an ideal birthday present for her would be and this is why.

4 What's your advice?

When you have read carefully all the pieces of information about **What's your advice?** do the following:

A

Answer the following questions in sentences.

1 What relation is Saloni Gavascar to the 75-year-old lady mentioned in the letter?
2 What is the main reason people over 65 value pets?
3 What is Oscar's pedigree?
4 Why do you think Walter would take a lot of looking after?
5 Do you think Mrs Gavascar would be able to leave her flat much? Give reasons for your answer.
6 What was Great Britain's third most popular pet in 1981?
7 What is one reason why pets are good for old people?
8 What is one of the things Mrs Gavascar enjoyed?
9 How long did it take Sue Tibble to answer Saloni's letter?
10 In which month of the year is Mrs Gavascar's birthday?

B

Bearing in mind what you know from reading all the pieces, do the following:

1 Write down the sort of things a pet might 'give you to talk about'.
2 Use your imagination and complete the letter Sue Tibble has started on the 1st July.
3 Discuss what you think Sue Tibble will recommend as the ideal pet – and then discuss what you think Saloni Gavascar and her mum and dad will think of the idea.

C

Write down what you think each of the following words means. Check with a dictionary to see if your definitions are correct.

value activities minor tempted ideal

D

Re-write the following passage. Fill in the blanks with what you think are suitable words. Check with the 'facts' when you need to.

The thing people over ____ like most about having a ____ is that it provides 24 hour companionship. This helps to stop them feeling ____ . Of course pets have to be looked after so it is important to choose the right ____ for somebody who cannot move about much. They should obviously not have a pet which needs a great deal of ____ .

E

Choose one of the following and with a friend, or friends, prepare either a short mime or play about it.

1 Gran's birthday.
2 Conducting a number of interviews with people to see what they most liked about having pets – and which are their favourite pets.
3 A scene in Sue Tibble's office when she and her assistants get the day's 'Problem Page' letters.
4 Finding the right home for Oscar.
5 Finding the right home for Walter.

F

1 Write a letter to Sue Tibble's 'Problem Page'. It could be about a problem which is actually worrying you – or it could be something entirely made up.
2 Use your imagination and write a dramatic story entitled: 'The day Star escaped'. 'Star' can be any kind of pet you choose to make it – remember there are plenty of pets other than dogs, cats and budgies!
3 Make two lists for yourself. In one write the advantages you think owning a pet would give you; in the second write down the disadvantages of owning a pet.

5 An opportunity lost

A

C

COMPETITION ENTRY FORM

Name:
Dee Senten

Address:
4 Pine Road
Brockley, Ossex.

Letter order:
B A C E D F G

Now send this form and your letter to:
Eat-a-Bix Breakfast Competition
PO Box 96
BLOGDEN

B

Eat-a-Bix Breakfast Competition,
P.O. Box 96,
Blogden.

4 Pine Road
Brockley,
Ossex.
3/3/88

Dear Sir,

Breakfast is the best meal of the day for me because it is the only meal I share with my mother. There are only the two of us living in my house because my mother is a widow. She has to go to work to keep us and doesn't get in until 7.30 pm at night.

At breakfast time she is always cheerful. She is not one of those people who are snappy and bad-tempered in the morning. I would very much like to win the holiday for her. She has not had a holiday for five years, although she saved up to send me ski-ing with the school last year.

Yours hopefully,
Dee Senten.

D

"A GREAT BREAKFAST" COMPETITION

Put the following in order of importance for having a "great breakfast". Write down letters only.

1st prize will go to the person who has letters in what we think is the best order – and has written the best letter about why "Breakfast is the Best Meal of the Day".

A Some fresh fruit
B A good, healthy cereal
C Toasted brown bread
D Marmalade or jam
E Plenty of tea to drink
F Some cooked food
G Good sauces

E

4th March 1988

BROCKLEY ARGUS

ACCIDENT OUTSIDE POST OFFICE

Dee Senton, a fourteen-year-old schoolgirl was taken to hospital suffering from shock and minor injuries after being hit by a motor cycle outside the High Street Post Office yesterday. She is expected to be in hospital for about a week.

"I'm quite all right really," said Dee to our reporter. "I was running to catch the post and didn't see the motor bike. Unfortunately I dropped a very important letter. It was blown away I suppose.

This letter

F

5th March, 1988

BROCKLEY ARGUS

MILLIONAIRE IN TOWN

Mr. V. B. King, one of the world's richest men is in town today. Mr. King, who made his fortune by inventing and manufacturing handy gadgets for the home, is known at home in the USA as "Mr. Christmas".

This is because every year he gives away hundreds of thousands of pounds to people in need, or who have suffered some kind of misfortune.

"One of the best things in my life," said Mr. King to our reporter, "is to be able to share my good fortune with other people."

5

An opportunity lost

When you have read carefully all the pieces of information about **An opportunity lost**, do the following:

A

Answer the following questions in sentences.

1 What is the 1st prize in the *Eat-a-bix* competition?
2 What do you have to do to win this prize?
3 Where can you find details about this competition?
4 With whom does Dee Senton have breakfast?
5 Can you say where one post office is situated in Brockley?
6 How did Mr King make his fortune?
7 What is his 'nickname'?
8 Does Mr King live in England?
9 What is the name of one newspaper in the town where Dee lives?
10 Is it likely that Dee would still be in hospital on 4th April, 1988?

B

Bearing in mind what you know from reading **An opportunity lost**, do the following:

1 The three most important people mentioned in this file are all generous and thoughtful. Write down a kindness you know each of them has done.
2 Look again at **E**. From what you know, write down what else you think Dee said to the *Brockley Argus* reporter.
3 Why do you think **B** might be a popular letter as first choice in the competition?

C

Write down what you think each of the following words means. Check with a dictionary to see if your definitions are correct.

cereal competition shock minor
inventing manufacturing gadgets misfortune

D

Re-write the following paragraph. Fill in the blanks with what you think are suitable words. Check with the 'facts' when you need to.

Dee has entered a competition in which she hopes to win a ____ day holiday for her mother. Mrs Senton's husband is ____ and she and Dee live together. Mrs Senton is ____ tempered in the morning, even though she has not had a ____ for five years. Dee went on a ____ sports holiday to ski. After her accident Dee was ____ enough to talk to a newspaper reporter. Mr V.B. King says that one of the best things in his life is ____ .

E

Choose one of the following and with a friend, or friends, prepare either a short mime or play about it.

1 What happened outside the post office when Dee had her accident.
2 How Mrs Senton got to know of Dee's accident.
3 The scene in the hospital when Dee's mother first visits her – and finds she is not badly hurt.

F

1 Do you think items **E** and **F** could have anything to do with each other in working out an ending for the 'story' of this file. Discuss this with your friends and then write out a newspaper article which might have appeared in the *Brockley Argus*, dated 6th March, 1988.
2 It is possible that this story could have a happy ending, which might be written under the title of 'The day I found a letter'. Can you write such a story?
3 Imagine you were the motor cyclist involved in the accident with Dee. Write a report of exactly what happened.
4 Imagine that Mr V.B. King visits Dee in hospital. What do you think they might talk about? Work out this conversation with a friend.

6 The pen pals

1 Pine View,
Benito,
California 631750,
U.S.A.
23rd April, 1988.

Hi Janice,

It was great to hear from you again last month – just think we have been writing to each other for two years now! I guess we must be real good "pen pals."

Well, now I will give you the latest news from sunny California. Daddy has just had the house repainted – all 50 rooms of it! The servants have all been very busy and it took ten men three weeks to do the job.

Did I tell you we have now got another Rolls Royce? Even though its only five minutes walk to our lovely private beach Daddy insists on taking us in the Rolls.

By the way thank you one million times for that lovely silk scarf you sent for my birthday. I was pretty lucky this year – got a speedboat from the folks!

I really wish we could get together sometime Janice – still it's great hearing from you.

Write soon pen pal! Love, Marsha XXX.

10 The Bungalows,
Sunley-on-Sea,
Burshire. 10/5/88

Dear Janice,

Now that I have moved from that big old house to this lovely bungalow by the sea I have decided to let all my grandchildren share my good fortune.

So pet here is a little surprise for you! I am sending you £300 and hope you can do something you really want with it.

I am looking forward to you coming to stay at Sunny Sunley sometime. Give my love to mum and dad.

Best wishes and fondest love, Gran

BARGAIN OF THE YEAR!
DON'T DELAY – FLY TODAY!

£299! RETURN FLIGHT

LONDON–BENITO, CALIFORNIA

AVAILABLE FOR AUGUST 1988 ONLY

DON'T MISS THIS ONE!

BAR-GAIN FLIGHTS
TEL: 020–37961

26A Ladyship Road
Bogley,
Smokeshire
1st June, 1988

Dear Marsha,

Fantastic news!! We can meet at last!! My grandmother has given me some money and I can get a flight out there to see you – isn't it wonderful?! You've said so often how you wished we could meet so I hope you will be as excited as I am. If you came here you'd have to share my bedroom with my sister and me – but as you've got 50 to choose from... I'm looking forward to seeing you – and your own beach – and the rocks – and just everything! Please hurry and write back and say that it will be all right if I come in August. I can't wait!

Love,
Janice xxx

6 The pen pals

When you have read carefully all the pieces of information about **The pen pals**, do the following:

A

Answer the following questions in sentences.

1. How long have Janice and Marsha been pen pals?
2. Judging by her letter does Marsha's family have one, or more, cars?
3. What 'special occasion' has Marsha had recently?
4. How do you think Gran is able to afford to give Janice £300?
5. Do you think the regular air fare from London to Benito would be more, or less, than £299 in July 1988?
6. Judging from her letter, do you think the children who live in Janice's house have a bedroom each?
7. What is the date on which Janice wrote to Marsha?
8. Which of the two letters addressed to Janice would you expect to take longer to reach her?
9. From the 'facts' it would appear that one of the letter writers is not telling the truth. Which one?
10. Look at the addresses on each letter. We can only be certain that one of these is at the seaside. Which one is it?

B

Bearing in mind what you know from reading **The pen pals** file, do the following:

1. Imagine you are Janice – write a letter back to Gran. Think carefully about the two things you would most probably want to tell her.
2. Look again at the picture of Marsha's home – and then her letter. Write down what you think are the main differences between what she says her home is like, and what it is really like.
3. Use your imagination and write down why you think Gran has moved.

C

Write down what you think each of the following words means. Check with a dictionary to see if your definitions are correct.

insists fortune bargain available delay

D

Re-write the following paragraph. Fill in the blanks with what you think are suitable words. Check with the 'facts' when you need to.

> The ____ letters shown in this 'file' tell an interesting story. For a start they show that ____ is a very generous person. They also show that ____ suddenly has enough money to fly to ____ . When we look at one of the letters and the picture we are almost certain that ____ is telling lies. It seems equally certain that if Janice were to see ____'s home she would get a big ____ .

E

Choose one of the following and with a friend, or friends, prepare either a short mime or play about it.

1 What happened when Janice received Gran's letter.
2 What happened when Marsha received Janice's letter.

F

1 Look again at Marsha's letter – and the picture of her house. Why do you think she might have made up the'fairy tale' about her house? Do you think she ever expected Janice to visit her? Discuss these and any other points you think of with your friends.
2 Imagine you are Marsha. You have got Janice's letter saying she is coming. What do you do – make up an excuse to persuade her not to come – tell her the truth – let her come without telling her the truth? Make your own decision here, and then write a letter to Janice.
3 Write the 'story' of this file and give it an ending. Think about this ending. Is Marsha finally truthful? Does Janice go to America? What happens when the two girls meet? Is there a happy ending – or an unhappy one?

7 Joke a minute

A

Viewpoints
BTV
Bilcaster

13 Pond Lane,
Arkfield
4.4.90

Dear Sir,

Seldom have I been so disgusted as I was when watching "Joke a Minute" last week.

Worst of all was Rob Bish. Not only were his jokes unfunny, but his continual face and hair pulling was extremely irritating.

I don't pay my television licence to

B

Viewpoints,
BTV,
Bilcaster

13 View Road
Arkfield,
4/4/90

Dear Sir,

I am writing to you about the performance of Rob Bish on "JOKE a Minute", last week. I thought it was absolutely great and I've never heard a comedian who had so many "with it" jokes. My friends and I couldn't stop laughing for the rest of the night. From all of us:–

MORE ROB BISH!

Thanks for the laughs,
yours faithfully,
Cilly Patter.

C

Viewpoints
BTV
Bilchester

Barley View
Hospital
Lynchfield
6/4/90

Dear Sir,

As the sister in charge of a busy hospital ward I don't usually have much time to write letters but I felt I just had to write this one.

There is no programme the patients in my ward look forward to more than "Joke a Minute". It is a delight to see them enjoying themselves so much – particularly when Rob Bish is on – where does he get all those corny jokes from?

Thank you for cheering up some very sick people.

Yours faithfully
Betty Barnes S.R.N.

D

Part of a script for Rob Bish and "stooge".

Bish: Do you know something . . .
Stooge: What?
Bish: My son goes to a very good school.
Stooge: Really?
Bish: Yes – they stopped him biting his finger nails on his first day there.
Stooge: Marvellous – how did they do that?
Bish: Knocked all his teeth out . . . talking of teeth I went for a meal last night.
Stooge: On yes?
Bish: The waiter said to me, 'How did you find your steak?'
Stooge: So . . .
Bish: Well I said to him, 'I just lifted up a chip and there it was'.

E

Rob Bish
"Hu Mer"
Oak Road,
Bilcaster.

BTV
Bilcaster
10th April, 1990

Dear Rob,

Good news! More people seem to like you than dislike you so we'd like you to do six more shows for us. Unfortunately we can only pay you 75% of what we did for the first series.

Yours ever,
Dirk Deal (Producer)
"Joke a Minute" – new series
May/June 1990.

F

Mr. R. Bish,
"Hu Mer",
Oak Road,
Bilcaster, England.

Valley Pines TV Group,
California 63217,
U.S.A.
10th April, 1990

Dear Mr. Bish,

Our representative saw your recent show on BTV. He said it was great – so we'd like you to do a series for us out here in California.

We'll double the fee BTV gave you, but you will need to spend May and June out here.

What do you say?

Best wishes,
Yours sincerely,

Bet Terdeal

Bet Terdeal

7 Joke a minute

When you have read carefully all the pieces of information about **Joke a minute**, do the following:

A

Answer the following questions in sentences.

1 Did the person from Pond Lane enjoy watching **Joke a minute**?
2 Did Cilly Patter watch **Joke a minute** by herself?
3 What does Rob Bish 'pull' during his act?
4 What is one programme which patients in Barley View Hospital enjoy?
5 What is Betty Barnes' job?
6 Why does Betty Barnes not write many letters?
7 What is Rob Bish's address?
8 Is there going to be another series of **Joke a minute**?
9 What has Dirk Deal got to do with **Joke a minute**?
10 Where does Miss Terdeal live?

B

Bearing in mind what you know from reading the **Joke a minute** file, do the following:

1 Write down the name of the letter writer who does not live in England.
2 If Rob Bish did another series of **Joke a minute** in May and June, would he earn more from this series than he did for the one in March and April?
3 Write out how you think letter **A** might finish – and invent a good name for the writer.
4 Having looked at the jokes in **D** can you carry this script on with a few more 'corny' jokes?

C

Write down what you think each of the following words means. Check with a dictionary to see if your definitions are correct.

continued irritating seldom script
stooge producer representative

D

Re-write the following paragraph. Fill in the blanks with what you think are suitable words. Check with the 'facts' when you need to.

The address to which people are writing about **Joke a minute** is ____ , BTV, Bilcaster. Letters **A** and **B** were both written on the 4th ____ . The patients who watch **Joke a minute** at Barley View hospital are not in good ____ . Dirk ____ has written to Rob Bish saying that ____ people liked his act than ____ it. One of the letters shown came from ____ in the United States of America.

E

1 With a friend practise the 'patter' between Rob Bish and his stooge. By the way you speak and use your voice, try to make the jokes as funny as possible. Try and continue to use a few jokes of your own.
2 Imagine that the writers of letters **A** and **B** met. What might they say to each other? Work out a conversation – it might get very argumentative!
3 With some friends imagine that you are interviewing some of the patients in Betty Barnes' hospital ward. Decide who will be the interviewer and who will be the patients – and get some opinions about **Joke a minute**. You might tape record your interviews.

F

1 What does SRN mean? Do some research and find out.
2 How old do you think the writer of letter **A** is? Discuss reasons for your opinion with your friends.
3 Look at letters **E** and **F** again. Which 'deal' do you think Rob Bish might accept? What might his reasons be? What are the advantages and disadvantages of each? Discuss these points with your friends.
4 Imagine you are Rob Bish. You have made up your mind whether **E** or **F** interests you most. Now write a letter to the one you accept.

8 Kidnap!

A

to EDitor
WoLvertoN STAr

WE Have goT EDWarD LItte. WE want £100,000 fOr HIS release.

INsTructions wILL BE TeLEPhoneD To YOU AT 8pm ON tuESDAY 30th MAY.

B

28th May

WOLVERTON STAR

MIDDAY "SNATCH" IN LORING STREET

by Roderick Freed

The city of Wolverton was shocked by a daring kidnapping at 12 noon today in Loring Street.

Rich businessman Edward Little was just leaving the VAL U department store, which he owns, when a dark blue Ford car screeched to a halt at the pavement.

Two men leapt out, seized Mr. Little and dragged him into the back of the car. Despite Mr. Little's desperate cries for help bystanders were too shocked to offer any assistance.

"Nobody even got the licence number," said

C

Wolverton to Aspen Motorway

FLATS

FLATS

FLATS

Viaduct Road

VAL U DEPARTMENT STORE

Entrance

NORTHERN BANK BUILDING

Bailey Street

EMDALE SHOPPING PRECINCT

Loring Street

Pimly Road

Graveyard

St Anselm's Church

MULTI-STOREY CAR PARK

Locarno Road

Key

• Traffic lights

N

D

FORM 131B
Police Report

Name, Rank, Number: 2529671 PC Charles Fox

Date of Report: 12-14pm. 28/5/86

Whilst on patrol in car 47 with PC Knowles we saw a blue Ford car proceeding east along Viaduct Road. This car was exceeding the speed limit. When we gave chase the car "jumped" the traffic lights at the junction between Viaduct Road and Bailey Street and turned north.

After "jumping" the lights again it turned east onto the Wolverton to Aspen Motorway. We continued to chase this car until

E

EDWARD LITTLE

Edward Little likes to call himself a "self made millionaire". He left school at 15 and set himself up with a market stall in Vest Lane market. Soon he controlled dozens of stalls in many Wolverton markets.

In 1974 he bought the building in Loring Street which is now the VAL U department store. Mr. Paul Lynch, owner of the building at that time said that he had been threatened, and his house vandalised, until he agreed to sell to Mr. Little. Mr. Little denied all knowledge of this.

After the fire in 1976, in which 3 people were killed in VAL U, Mr. Little was fined for not taking the proper fire precautions. Mrs. Val Thyme, a department manager who was sacked after the fire, said that Mr. Little was "the worst person she had ever known in her life".

F

29/5/86 Transcript of a TV interview with Mr. Geoffrey Pike.

Interviewer: "Mr Pike - you have been known as the person who knows Mr Little better than anyone else."

Pike: "I don't know about that, but I have known him since we were boys."

Interviewer: "Is it true that Mr Little is not the most popular of men?"

Pike: "Some people might say that - I like him."

Interviewer: "What is your present job Mr Pike?"

Pike: "Since 1977, general manager of VAL U department store?"

Interviewer: "Is it true you were in prison for fraud in 1969 Mr Pike?"

Pike: "I don't see what that has to do with what we are talking about. No more questions. No - that's it!"

8 Kidnap!

When you have read carefully all the pieces of information about **Kidnap!** do the following:

A

Answer the following questions in sentences.

1 At what time do the kidnappers intend to telephone more instructions?
2 Where was Mr Little coming from when he was kidnapped?
3 Why did no-one go to help Mr Little at this time?
4 What building is due south of the VAL U department store?
5 What were the names of the policemen in car 47?
6 What caused the policemen to chase the blue Ford?
7 Why do you think Mr Paul Lynch might have sold the building on Loring Street to Mr Little?
8 Why was Mr Little fined in 1976?
9 Why do you think Geoffrey Pike likes Mr Little?
10 Can you think of one kind deed which Mr Little has done?

B

Bearing in mind what you know from reading all the pieces, do the following:

1 Complete the newspaper report in **B** in your own words.
2 Complete the police report in **D** in your own words.
3 Re-draw the map **C** – and put in the route which you know the getaway car followed.

C

Write down what you think each of the following words means. Check with a dictionary to see if your definitions are correct.

bystanders exceeding junction vandalised denied precautions fraud

D

Re-write the following paragraph. Fill in the blanks with what you think are suitable words. Check with the 'facts' when you need to.

Mr Edward Little has so much money that he is a ____ . He has been very successful although he left ____ at 15.

Despite being successful he does not seem to have been a very ____ man. One lady described him as the ____ person she had ever known in her life. Mr Little has ____ good friend in Geoffrey Pike. The first person to hear of Mr Little's kidnap was the ____ of the *Wolverton Star*.

E

Choose one of the following and with a friend, or friends, prepare either a short mime or play about it.

1 The scene when Mr Little was kidnapped.
2 What happened when the ransom note was delivered to the newspaper office.
3 What happened inside the police car when the speeding Ford was sighted.
4 Further interviews with Mr Lynch and Mrs Thyme.

F

1 Write out a 'character study' of Mr Little. Study all the facts you know about him and then write your opinion about him.
2 Look again at the evidence given. Then discuss with your friends who you think might have organised this kidnapping. Give reasons for your choice.

9 Leaving early?

22 Duneln Street,
Fishley
Thursday. 26/10/86

Dear Mrs Marshall,

As you know Maureen has been having a lot of pain with her teeth this week. I have finally been able to make an appointment for her at the dentist. Could she therefore please leave school at 2.30 pm this afternoon?

Yours sincerely,

S. M. Briggs.

FISHLEY SCHOOL REPORT

PUPIL'S NAME: Maureen Briggs DATE OF REPORT: July '86

Social behaviour: Maureen is pleasant and charming. She is also very keen on getting her own way and will often take daring steps to achieve this.

Involvement in school activities: Maureen is a marvellous actress. She can mime and "act a part" quite brilliantly. She will take part in plays but prefers doing things by herself. She is very good at all physical activities.

Academic progress: Maureen is very intelligent but makes excellent progress only when she concentrates. She is also very clever with her hands – has copied some old manuscript writing quite beautifully. She writes with imagination.

Parent's comments: I am please with Maureen report. She never tells me nothing about school. She does like her own way though. Excuse my English but I am just learning it.

Parent's signature: S.M. Briggs

Teacher's signature: C. Phillpotts

Miss Maureen Briggs,
22 Dunelm St.,
Fishley
Ref: IC/PT/4

B. FIT Ltd.,
77 High Street,
Fishley
15/10/86

Dear Miss Briggs,

Please find enclosed with this letter the ice skates which were your prize for the amateur skating competition win at Fishley Rink last month.

Congratulations on your success! We hope you will continue your enjoyment on ice – and that our skates will help.

LOAMSHIRE COUNTY COUNCIL

Dental Inspection Card

Place of inspection: Fishley School

Date: 3/10/86 *Child's name:* Maureen Briggs

Result:

1. Your child needs dental treatment and an appointment will be made when you return this card. ☐
2. Your child's teeth and gums are healthy. ☑

FISHLEY NURSERIES

List of Employees.

Name	Address	Tel. No.	Shift.
ARTHUR J.B	14 Tusker Court, Fishley	21731	8am - 2pm
ASKEN P.	23 Endleigh St., Fishley	31452	8am - 2pm
BARTON L.W.	16 Dean Drive, Downton	770 - 62131	2pm - 8pm
BRIGGS S.M.	22 Durelm St., Fishley	54971	2pm - 8pm
CHARLTON T.	45A Kane Court, Downton	770 - 21211	8am - 2pm
DONNE S.	103 Reed Road, Fishley	39756	8am - 2pm
ELVIN F.W.	10 High Rd., Fishley	43501	2pm - 8pm.

THE STAR'S WHAT'S ON SPOT

WEEK ENDING 29th OCTOBER

ALFREDO'S

Eat out at Alf's on Monday nights and get 2 meals for the price of one.

Ring 76761 for details

LADIES!
KEEP FIT–NOT FAT!
Birdie McQueen's classes are every Tuesday & Friday
53214 for more info

DON'T MISS IT!

WORLD ICE SKATING STARS

DOSSOM & BLEARY

ARE GIVING A MATINEE CONCERT AT 3 PM ON THURSDAY 26th OCTOBER IN THE FISHLEY ICE RINK. YOUR ONLY CHANCE TO SEE THE WORLD'S GREATEST!

THE EXODUS ROCK BAND

plays in the Drill Hall
Friday at 7 pm
All welcome

Dog trainer's group

Weds. at 7 pm

Oakleigh School

9 Leaving early?

When you have read carefully all the pieces of information about **Leaving early?** do the following:

A

Answer the following questions in sentences.

1 What is the time and date of Maureen's dental appointment?
2 Do you think Maureen is good at PE? Give reasons for your answer.
3 Does Maureen make 'excellent progress' all the time?
4 What are the names of the World Ice Skating stars?
5 Can Maureen ice skate?
6 Can you name one shop in Fishley High Street?
7 What was the result of Maureen's last school dental inspection?
8 Where does Maureen's mother work?
9 Could she be contacted by telephone at home on a weekday at 3pm?
10 Is Mrs Briggs normally free from work at the time Maureen has her dental appointment?

B

Bearing in mind what you know from reading the **Leaving early?** file, do the following:

1 Write down the date of Maureen's last dental inspection; the time her mother is at work; the time and date the letter says Maureen has an appointment.
2 Write down the only item in the *What's On* advertisement which takes place on the same day as Maureen's dental appointment.
3 How do you think the letter from B. Fit Ltd. would end?

C

Write down what you think each of the following words means. Check with a dictionary to see if your definitions are correct.

achieve prefers physical manuscript matinee amateur employees

D

Re-write the following paragraph. Fill in the blanks with what you think are suitable words. Check with the 'facts' when you need to.

Maureen's report says that she is pleasant and ____ . She is also very good at using her____ and is skilful at copying manuscript ____ . It is surprising that Maureen is having problems with her ____ because she has recently had a satisfactory dental examination. Mrs Briggs cannot write English as well as her daughter ____ . The name of Maureen's present ____ is Mrs Marshall.

E

Choose one of the following and with a friend, or friends, prepare either a short mime or play about it.

1 What happened when Maureen received the parcel from B. Fit Ltd.?
2 What did Maureen and her mother say to each other when they discussed Maureen's school report at home?
3 What happened at the school dental inspection?

F

1 Look again at all the evidence in this file. Do you think Mrs Briggs really wrote the note of 26th October? What evidence is there to suggest that she did not? If not who *did* write it, and why? Discuss all these points with your friends.
2 Imagine that the headteacher of Fishley School had to take some further action about this note. Who would she see? What might she do? What might be the consequences?

10 Four seats please

The Manager, Box Office,
Orville Theatre
Princess Road,
Smirkley.

24 Hope Drive,
Smirkley

1st October

Dear Sir,

I saw your advertisement for the Charlie Greaves show and I would like to book 4 tickets.

I would like 4 £6 stall tickets for the Saturday Matinee on 15th October. My mother has a stiff leg so it would be much appreciated if one of these seats could be at the end of a row.

Please find a postal order for £24 enclosed and a stamped addressed envelope for you to use.

Yours faithfully,

N. Joy

You won't snigger.
You won't even giggle.
You'll ROAR
with laughter at

THE CHARLIE GREAVES SHOW!

2 hours of fun, music and fantasy.

ORVILLE THEATRE, SMIRKLEY

10th–15th OCTOBER
8 pm nightly
Matinées Wed/Sat at 2 p.m.
All seats bookable

£7; £6; £5.50; £3

For reservations write to
BOX OFFICE
ORVILLE THEATRE
PRINCESS ROAD
SMIRKLEY

Row	Seats		
H	1 2 3 4 5 6 7 8 9 10 11 12 13 14 15 16	17 18 19 20 21 22 23 24 25 26 27 28 29 30 31	
G	1 2 3 4 5 6 7 8 9 10 11 12 13 14 15 16	17 18 19 20 21 22 23 24 25 26 27 28 29 30 31	
F	1 2 3 4 5 6 7	8 9 10 11 12 13 14	
E	1 2 3 4 5 6 7	8 9 10 11 12 13 14	15 16 17 18 19 20 21
D	1 2 3 4 5 6 7	8 9 10 11 12 13 14	15 16 17 18 19 20 21
C	1 2 3 4 5 6 7	8 9 10 11 12 13 14	15 16 17 18 19 20 21
B	1 2 3 4 5 6 7	8 9 10 11 12 13 14	15 16 17 18 19 20 21
A	1 2 3 4 5 6 7	8 9 10 11 12 13 14	15 16 17 18 19 20 21
			15 16 17 18 19 20 21

STAGE

H	= £3
G	= £5.50
E/F	= £6
A/B/C/D	= £7

ORVILLE THEATRE SEAT PLAN

N. Joy,
24 Hope Drive,
Smirkley

Orville Theatre,
Princess Road,
Smirkley
4/10/88

Dear Sir/Madam,

It was impossible to book an end row seat as you requested. Otherwise the tickets (E3,4,5,6) are exactly as you asked.

Yours faithfully,

Mayda Blunder

Mayda Blunder
Box Office Manager

Mr T. Rouble,
1 Nim Walk,
Smirkley

Orville Theatre,
Princess Road,
Smirkley
4/10/88

Dear Mr Rouble,

Please find your tickets - E3,4,5,6 for 8pm on 15/10/88 enclosed.

Yours faithfully,

Mayda Blunder

Mayda Blunder
Box Office Manager

ORVILLE THEATRE

PERFORMANCE:
8 pm 15/10/88
£6

Always check your ticket!

ROW E Seat 3

ROW E Seat 4

ROW E Seat 5

ROW E Seat 6

10 Four seats please

When you have read carefully all the pieces of information about **Four seats please**, do the following:

A

Answer the following questions in sentences.

1 Who do you think is the star of the show at the Orville Theatre on 5–10th October?
2 How much would two of the cheapest seats cost?
3 How many nights is the show on?
4 What is the total number of performances to be given?
5 Why does N. Joy's mother want an end seat?
6 How has N. Joy paid for the four tickets?
7 How much would seats **D 10**, **11**, and **12** cost all together?
8 Can you think of one reason why seat **H 15** is cheaper than seat **A 10**?
9 Who is Mayda Blunder?
10 Do you think there are any musicians in the Charlie Greaves Show?

B

Bearing in mind what you know from reading all these pieces, do the following:

1 Draw the row in which N. Joy's seats are, then shade in the seats booked by N. Joy.
2 Draw and complete the front of 'the stamped addressed envelope' which N. Joy sent to the Orville Theatre.
3 If every seat in the Orville Theatre was sold at the prices advertised, what would the total sum of money taken be?

C

Write down what you think each of the following words means. Check with a dictionary to see if your definitions are correct.

reservations **advertisement** **appreciated**
check **requested** **performances**

D

Re-write the following paragraph. Fill in the blanks with what you think are suitable words. Check with the 'facts' when you need to.

We know from the advertisement that the Charlie Greaves Show ____ for two hours, and that the Orville Theatre can be ____ in Princess Road. N. Joy's letter is dated ____ weeks and ____ day before the show for which seats are being booked. We can see from the tickets that the seats given are in the ____ row from the front. Row **D** would be the ____ row from the back. Mayda ____'s letter is dated ____ days after the one written by N. Joy.

E

Choose one of the following and with a friend, or friends, prepare either a short mime or play about it.

1 A comedy routine from the Charlie Greaves Show.
2 What happened in the Box Office when N. Joy's letter arrived.
3 What happened when Mayda Blunder's letter arrived at 24 Hope Drive.
4 What *might* happen at the 8pm performance on 15th October.

F

1 Write out why Mayda Blunder addressed N. Joy as 'Sir/Madam' instead of Mr, Mrs, Miss or Ms.
2 'Mayda Blunder' is the name given to the Box Office Manager for obvious reasons if you look carefully at all the 'facts'. What blunders have been made? How might they be put right? What could the consequences be? Can you think why they have happened in the first place? Discuss these points with your friends.
3 Imagine you are N. Joy. You get Mayda Blunder's letter and the tickets. You check them. How do you feel? Next write a letter back to Mayda Blunder – think carefully about exactly what you will say in it.

11 Letters to the editor

A

26 The Views,
Herland.

The Editor,
'The Herland Echo',
Fore Street,
Herland.

24th May.

Dear Sir,

I have heard of overcrowding on buses and trains - but aeroplanes! Whilst flying home from a business trip last week I saw a sight I am not likely to forget.

Fortunately I had my camera with me and took a photograph. I enclose this photograph with this letter so that you can see what I mean.

Surely it would be much safer to give all airline passengers a seat - rather than let them stand on the wings - even if they have parachutes!

Yours sincerely,
Con Cerned

B

The Editor,
"The Herland Echo,"
Fore Street,
Herland

14 Arkley Place,
Bassett.
24th May

Dear Sir,

I hope you will print this letter because it is about one of the most sensible things I have seen for a long time. I have always wondered why travellers in aeroplanes were not given parachutes.

Last week I saw a small airliner which was obviously in some sort of difficulty. All the passengers however had their parachutes on and had climbed out ready to jump to safety.

Yours faithfully,

Gull Ible

C

The Editor,
"The Herland Echo,"
Fore Street,
Herland

Dear Sir,

I want to tell you about my dad's hobby. He is a member of the Herland Free Fall Parachute Team. On a "Jump" day this is what happens . . . .

Yours faithfully
John Boyle (aged 12)

D

The Editor,
'The Herland Echo',
Fore Street,
Herland

'Homeleigh',
Herland,

24 May

Dear Sir,

I am writing to protest about these people who keep jumping out of the sky. Last week I was doing my garden when I heard a shout. There was a man in a flying suit sort of thing, all tied up in a parachute, clinging to my chimney pot!

So . . . .

Yours complainingly,
I. Grouse

11 Letters to the editor

When you have read carefully all the pieces of information about **Letters to the editor** do the following:

A

Answer the following questions in sentences.

1 From where do you think Con Cerned took his photograph?
2 Where had Con Cerned been?
3 What are the home towns of the letter-writers?
4 What is the name of the only letter-writer whose name we know?
5 How many of the letters are 'protests'?
6 Which of the letter-writers do you think knows most about what goes on in the aeroplane in the photograph?
7 If you were the editor, what would you think about the person who wrote Letter **A**?
8 Which is the letter which describes an accidental happening?
9 Why do you think this is rather an unusual collection of 'Letters to the Editor'?
10 Do you think some of these letters are *not* really serious? If so, say which ones and why.

B

Bearing in mind what you know from reading all these pieces, do the following:

1 Complete John Boyle's letter. Think carefully about what you might write here.
2 Write what you think happens inside the plane before anybody climbs out of it.
3 Imagine you are the editor of the *Herland Echo*. Write a letter back to John Boyle and tell him why you think his letter has been particularly useful.

C

Write down what you think each of the following words means. Check with a dictionary to see if your definitions are correct.

enclose concerned gullible grouse protest

D

Re-write the following paragraph. Fill in the blanks with what you think are suitable words. Check with the 'facts' when you need to.

The photograph could only have been taken by somebody who was either flying in another ____ , or drifting down on a ____ . All the people who can be seen in the photograph have ____ on their heads. Only ____ of the letter-writers actually claims that they saw this plane. It is possible that one of the men seen on the plane could be Mr ____ .

E

Choose one of the following and with a friend or friends, prepare either a short mime or play about it.

1. Imagine you were in an airliner which suddenly came alongside the aeroplane in the photograph. What happens? What do people say? What do they do?
2. Act out the story of I. Grouse and the parachutist who lands on the roof.
3. How might Mr Boyle describe an adventure of the Free Fall Team to John?

F

1. Describe how you think the parachutist came to land round a chimney rather than in the landing zone. You could write this as if it was happening to you.
2. Look again at Letters **A** and **B**. Now try and write another funny/outrageous/ridiculous letter to the editor, saying why these men were outside the plane – because they felt sick; because it was crowded inside; because they could travel cheaper; because they got a better view – **use your imagination**!

12 Making a choice

SPACE NEWS

AUTUMN EDITION

The recent accident at the Space Probe Centre showed the value of the cadet training course. When the "mock-up" of an interplanetary air bus caught fire, 16-year-old Cadet Linda Phillips acted with great courage and initiative.

Leaping into the capsule she pulled aside the unconscious pilot and triggered the computerised fire extinguishers. She then . . .

WANTED
TRAINEE SPACESHIP CREW
1 VACANCY

Due to promotion of one of our older cadets there is a vacancy at Space Probe Centre for a trainee cadet. Full training and education will be given. Applicant should be between 12 and 16.

Apply to Marc Zeal, Training Officer, Space Probe Centre, LF191.

Remember: be honest, but tell us as FULLY as possible why you think you should be chosen for this post. Give the name of one person who we can ask about you.

Marc Zeal, Training Off Space Probe

Ted Lotus 15 Napier Road
Oldfield Splint

Hi Man!

Looking for a Trainee Space Cadet - I'm your man! 16 years old - into pop music, computers, poeple, adventure! I used to play soccer and do wieght training - led a grupp to Oldfield.

Somebody who will tell you more is Wally Field 16 Napier Road

Heres hopeing for the best

Cheers T.L.

Marc Zeal,
Training Officer,
Space Probe Centre,
LF191

12 Briar Lane Road,
Coatley
Durshire
22.11.99

Dear Sir,

I would like to apply for training at the Space Probe Centre in order to become a Space Crew member.

My details are:

1. 14 years old
2. Academic interests: Maths, Science, Computers. I have spent a lot of time working with KAPITAN and CAPAL computers.
3. Other interests: Swimming, games, judo.
4. Qualifications: I have got several efficiency badges through being a member of Brownies and Guides.

My mother died when I was 10 years old and I have had to help my father look after the family. My older sister has now returned home however so I could start training at once.

For more details about me you could contact: Alistair Green, Warden, Coatley Adventure Centre, Durshire EN6 750.

Yours faithfully

Sue Fayne

Marc Zeal,
Training Officer,
Space Probe Centre,
LF 191.

12 Briar Lane Road,
Coatley,
Durshire,
22/11/99

Dear Sir,

Trainee Spaceship Crew

I saw your advertisement for the above and I would like to apply.

I am 13 years of age and very fit. I have been captain of the junior school netball team and am a medal winning swimmer. I have worked with computers both at home and at school, knowing best the KAPITAN 64 with the 66 Key QWERTY keyboard.

I like Space Cadet's uniforms.

Yours sincerely,

Zelda Partridge

Marc Zeal
Training Officer,
Space Probe Centre,
LF 191

Flat 2A.
Pimley Place,
Zetland,
22/11/99

Dear Mr Zeal,

I would like to apply to be a cadet at Space Probe Centre. I am 12 years old and at the moment I go to Appledore Comprehensive School. I don't like it here and would like to move.

I am interested in Maths. P.E. the Boy's Brigade and Basketball.

My Dad will answer more questions about me.

Yours sincerely,

Oliver Potts.

CONFIDENTIAL

TRAINING OFFICER
TRAINEE SPACESHIP PROGRAMME.

The candidate chosen should have as many of the following qualifications as possible:

1. *Should be between 12 and 16; boy or girl; very fit.*
1. *Needs to be agile and quick thinking.*
2. *Needs to be agile and quick thinking.*
3. *Should be able to write neatly and keep good notes.*
4. *Should have some knowledge of computers.*
5. *Should be prepared to wear a uniform.*
6. *Should be prepared to take responsibility.*

12 Making a choice

When you have read carefully all the pieces of information about **Making a choice**, do the following:

A

Answer the following questions in sentences.

1 Who acted with 'great courage and initiative'?
2 Why is there one vacancy for training at the Space Probe Centre?
3 What is the minimum age at which you can apply for this post?
4 What tells us that Ted Lotus should be fit and agile?
5 Is Sue Fayne an only child?
6 Both Sue Fayne and Zelda Partridge are familiar with which computer?
7 Which of the letter-writers went to Appledore School?
8 Which of the letter-writers are interested in swimming?
9 Do you think that the letter-writers know about the 'list of qualifications' needed for the post?
10 What did Linda Phillips do at the accident to show that she was agile?

B

Bearing in mind what you know from reading the **Making a choice** file, do the following:

1 Write down the name of the letter-writer who you know has worn a uniform.
2 Write down the name of the letter-writer about whose handwriting you know very little.
3 What is it in *Space News* which shows that a knowledge of computers is important?
4 Which of the candidates do you think has had to take most responsibility in his or her life?

C

Write down what you think each of the following words means. Check with a dictionary to see if your definitions are correct.

initiative vacancy qualifications agile candidate efficiency

D

Re-write the following paragraph. Fill in the blanks with

what you think are suitable words. Check with the 'facts' when you need to.

The applicants for the space cadetship include ____ boys and ____ girls. ____ ____ is the oldest of the applicants, and only one definitely attends a ____ school. Two of the candidates come from ____ in Durshire and ____ ____ has forgotten to put a date on his letter.

E

Choose one of the following and with a friend, or friends, prepare either a short mime or play about it.

1 Act out the accident at the Space Probe Centre.
2 Preparing it carefully beforehand, work out an 'interview' between Marc Zeal and Ted Lotus.

F

1 Look again at the report in *Space News*. Next, use your imagination and continue the report to tell what happened next.
2 Look again at all the applicants' letters – and the qualifications list. Discuss with your friends who you think is the best candidate? What are the points which make him or her so? Is another candidate a close second best? What are the weaknesses of the worst letter/letters?
3 Imagine you are Marc Zeal. You have to write to the best candidate saying that you wish to interview him/her at two o'clock in the afternoon of 10th December, 1999 in Room 53 of the Space Probe Centre. Now write this letter.

13 Help!

17/7/95

To: The Editor
Daily Globe
New York City

Sir

I hope you will print this letter in your paper because it is a challenge to SUPERMAN!

As a private investigator I have been on the trail of one of the world's greatest criminals for several months. I now believe that Ronald Dakin, "lost" since the great $1000,000 gold robbery is hiding out in England. I intend to go there and make sure he is arrested.

Perhaps Superman is not the world's greatest crime fighter when a simple detective can get these results!

Yours faithfully
Louise Powers.

27-7-95 9.19pm
2,000 MILES OUT OVER THE ATLANTIC, AT A HEIGHT OF 30,000 FEET...
AIR FORCE 1: "THIS IS AIR FORCE 1 TO BASE...OVER".
BASE: "GO AHEAD AIR FORCE 1. RECEIVING YOU LOUD AND CLEAR. OVER."
AIR FORCE 1: "THIS IS TO REPORT AN UNIDENTIFIED FLYING OBJECT MOVING AT FANTASTIC SPEED. TRAVELLING FROM WEST TO EAST AT 30,000 FT. OVER."
BASE: "ROGER AIR FORCE 1 WE PICKED UP THE UFO BRIEFLY ON OUR RADAR. OVER AND OUT."
WE INTERRUPT THIS PROGRAMME TO BRING YOU AN URGENT MESSAGE. AN UNIDENTIFIED FLYING OBJECT HAS BEEN SIGHTED FLYING OVER LONDON...
NEWS FLASH
27-7-95 9.20 pm local time

13 Help!

When you have read carefully all the pieces of information about **Help!** do the following:

A

Answer the following questions in sentences.

1 How much time has past between Louise Powers' letter – and the scene 'somewhere off the east coast of England'?
2 What is the name of the criminal mentioned?
3 Who do you think the man throwing the 'package' might be?
4 Who do you think is in the 'package'?
5 What is the UFO sighted by Air Force 1?
6 Why is the UFO travelling from west to east?
7 How long has it taken the UFO to travel from mid-Atlantic to London?
8 Who is Louise Powers hoping will rescue her?
9 If Superman attempts to rescue Louise, from where will he have to rescue her?
10 How much time do you think is left to make the rescue?

B

Bearing in mind what you know from reading all the pieces, do the following:

1 Write down (in story form if you like) what you think has happened between 17/7/95 and 27/7/95 in Louise Powers' life.
2 Write what you think Ronald Dakin must be feeling at 9.18pm on 27/7/95.
3 Imagine you are the pilot of Air Force 1. Write out a conversation you might have with your best friend when you get back to base. Make it all about the fantastic sight you have seen.

C

Write down what you think each of the following words means. Check with a dictionary to see if your definitions are correct.

investigator challenge unidentified briefly local

D

Re-write the following paragraph. Fill in the blanks with what you think are suitable words. Check with the facts when you need to.

Louise Powers hopes that ____ will ____ the *Daily Globe*. If he does he will see the letter in which she makes a ____ to him. From the picture showing the east coast of England it seems likely that ____ ____ found ____ ____ . Louise is in trouble as a result and makes a plea to ____ for ____ . From the pilot's report and the TV announcer's statement it seems that ____ is coming to the ____ .

E

Choose one of the following and, with a friend or friends, prepare either a short mime or play about it.

1 What happened before the scene at 'the east coast of England'.
2 What happened at 9.21pm.
3 How Ronald Dakin is finally caught.

F

1 Write out the conversation which takes place between Louise and Superman if the rescue is successful. When you have worked out this conversation practise it with a friend and then tape record it, trying to make it sound 'live'.
2 Imagine that it is a month after all these events have taken place. Louise Powers decides she will write another letter to the *Daily Globe*. Use your imagination, think what she might want to say this time, and then write the letter.
3 Draw a strip cartoon (with words) which tells this whole story in comic form.

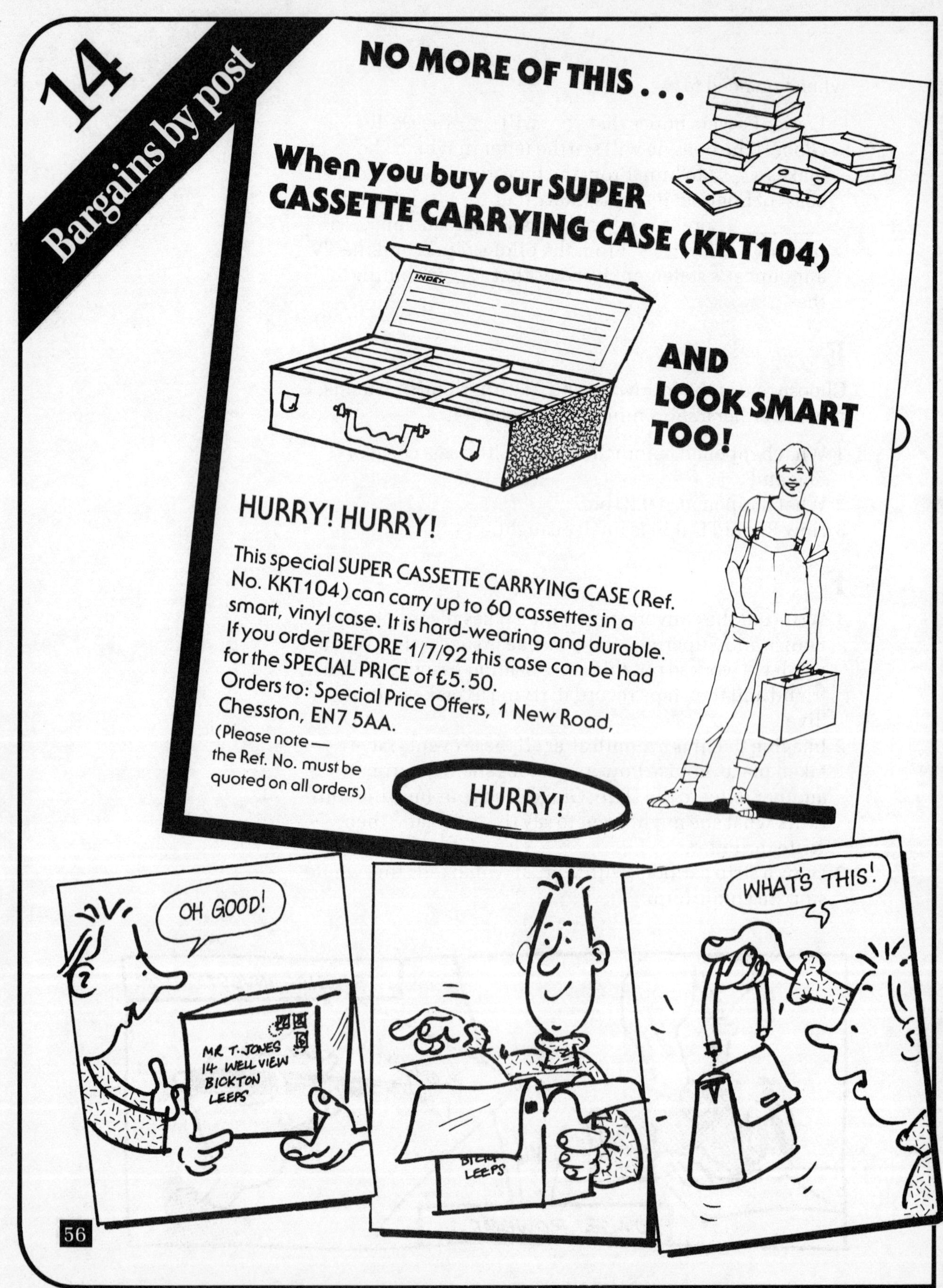
14
Bargains by post
NO MORE OF THIS . . .
When you buy our SUPER CASSETTE CARRYING CASE (KKT104)
INDEX
AND LOOK SMART TOO!
HURRY! HURRY!
This special SUPER CASSETTE CARRYING CASE (Ref. No. KKT104) can carry up to 60 cassettes in a smart, vinyl case. It is hard-wearing and durable. If you order BEFORE 1/7/92 this case can be had for the SPECIAL PRICE of £5.50.
Orders to: Special Price Offers, 1 New Road, Chesston, EN7 5AA.
(Please note — the Ref. No. must be quoted on all orders)
HURRY!
OH GOOD!
MR T. JONES
14 WELL VIEW
BICKTON
LEEPS
LEEPS
WHAT'S THIS!

Special Price Offers,
1 New Road,
Cherston,
EN7 5AA.

Trevor Jones,
14 Well View,
Bickton.
Leeps.
26/6/92.

Dear Sirs,

Super Cassette Carrying Case.
(Ref. No. TKK 104).

Please send me one of the above.
I enclose a postal order for £5.50 to cover the cost of this.

Yours faithfully,

Trevor Jones.

Special Price Offers,
1 New Road,
Cherston,
EN7 5AA.

Trevor Jones.
14 Well View,
Bickton,
Leeps.
15/7/92.

Dear Sirs,

I wish to protest most strongly!
I ordered one of your Super Cassette Carrying Cases at the special price of £5.50.
I quoted the reference number; I ordered before 1/7/92; I enclosed the correct amount of money.
Despite this I received on 10th July a LADIES HANDBAG!
I would be glad to hear your explanation of this - and what you intend to do about it.

Yours faithfully,
Trevor Jones

14 Bargains by post

When you have read carefully all the pieces of information about **Bargains by post**, do the following:

A

Answer the following questions in sentences.

1 What is the reference number for the Super Cassette Carrying Case?
2 How many cassettes would it carry when full?
3 By which date have orders to be received in order to qualify for the special price?
4 Would you think that this case is normally cheaper or more expensive than £5.50?
5 What is the cassette case made of?
6 Did Trevor Jones post his letter in time to qualify for the special price?
7 When did he receive the parcel from Special Price Offers?
8 Would you say that Trevor Jones' second letter was one of appreciation, concern or anger?
9 What does Trevor Jones ask for in his second letter?
10 What do you think he expects Special Price Offers to do?

B

Bearing in mind what you know from reading all the pieces, do the following:

1 Write down two lists of words. In the first write the feelings Trevor Jones might have felt when he saw the parcel waiting for him – in the second list write the feelings he might have experienced after he opened the parcel.
2 Write down why you think he got a handbag instead of a case – remember to check the facts before you give your answer!
3 Imagine the conversation Trevor might have had with his best friend when he received the handbag. Write out this conversation and then, with a friend, tape record it. Try to get plenty of expression into it.

C

Write down what you think each of the following words means. Check with a dictionary to see if your definitions are correct.

durable vinyl quoted enclose reference

D

Re-write the following paragraph. Fill in the blanks with what you think are suitable words. Check with the facts when you need to.

Trevor Jones was ____ when he saw a cassette carrying case for a cheap price. When he received his parcel however he was ____ . He sat down and wrote a strong letter of ____ to Special Price Offers. Trevor was particularly angry because he claimed that he had done everything ____ when sending for the case. He wanted to know how the ____ had been made.

E

Choose one of the following and, with a friend or friends, prepare either a short mime or play about it.

1 What happened when Trevor's second letter was received at Special Price Offers. You might start as follows:

Secretary: *You've got a letter of complaint here Mr Luke.*

Mr Luke: *Complaint? What about? Let's have a look.*

2 Trevor, along with a friend, opening the parcel.

F

1 Write a letter back from Special Price Offers in which Mr Luke makes his comments.

2 Decide for yourself how all this is finally settled. Write down the details.

3 Write out a one-sided telephone conversation in which Trevor explains the whole story to somebody. Write down only what Trevor says. Then give your book to a friend and ask him or her if they can work out what the person on the other end of the line says.

15 Message from the past

P. 29

The Mysteries Box.

Message from the Past

1. *Take one sheet of the Mysteries Box special paper.*
2. *Crumple paper thoroughly in hand.*
3. *Press paper out flat.*
4. *Singe edges of paper. (See instructions P.50).*
5. *Use special Mysteries Box ink and pen and write message.*

WHAT WILL YOUR MYSTERIES BOX MESSAGE SAY?

Mr Alfred Noble,
22, Heath Lane.
SPONDON.
SP14 4DQ.

December 20th

Dear Alf,

Thank you for your kindness to me over the past year. Now that I can walk again I hope to come round and see you soon. I never thought a game of football would cause me such trouble.

When I come round I will be bringing two bottles for your antique collection. They are very old and I hope you will find them interesting. Hope Maggie and young Keith are well.

Best wishes,
Jock.

14th January

BLEESTON ARGUS

FOUND!

At 6 pm on Monday Mital Patel found an unusual bottle on Bleeston Beach.

Being a student of history Mr. Patel knew that an ancient law dating from Queen Elizabeth I's reign forbids finders to open found, sealed bottles.

As a result the bottle was kept at Bleeston Police Station until a representative of Her Majesty's Government came to open it and examine the message inside.

"This is a most interesting find", said Mr. Hugh Hawes-Brown. "The bottle is at least two hundred years old and I think the message is . . .

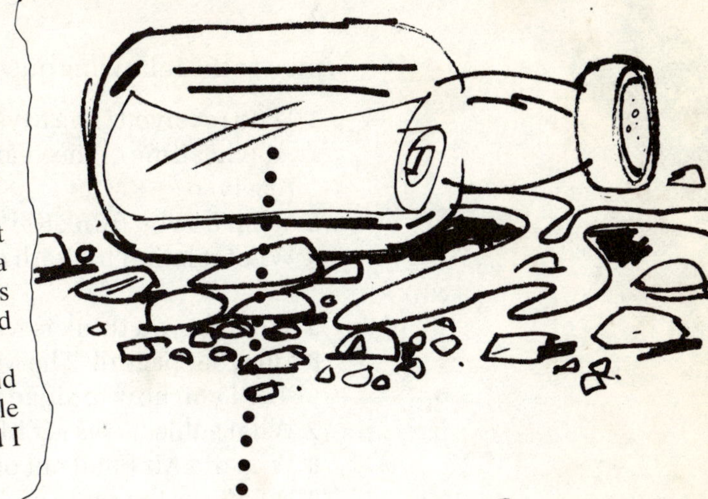

Help! We are the good ship "WITZ" full of gold and bound for Hamburg from W. Indies. On fire and sinking 10 miles NNW of trinidad. Taking to the boats. God be with us.

Dear Uncle Fred, 22nd January, Our Place.

You are the only person I feel I can ask for advice - because mum is always saying "What a lad" you were when you were young. Well, I think there's going to be some real trouble if I don't do something quickly!!!

Perhaps I had better start by telling you the whole story...

15 Message from the past

When you have read carefully all the pieces of information about **Message from the past**, do the following:

A

Answer the following questions in sentences.

1 Who received 'The Mysteries Box' as a present?
2 At what time of the year do you think this present was received?
3 What do you think Keith's surname is?
4 What relation to Keith do you think Mr Alfred Noble is?
5 What do you think is Keith's mother's name?
6 On what page of 'The Mysteries Box' instructions does it tell you how to singe paper?
7 What subject was Mr Mital Patel studying?
8 Why did Mr Patel not open the bottle?
9 What was the route of the ship mentioned in 'the message'?
10 Who do you think was writing the letter to Uncle Fred?

B

Bearing in mind what you know from reading the **Message from the past** file, do the following:

1 Write down the name of the person we *know* is aware that Alf Noble has a collection of antique bottles.
2 Write down the name of the person who will have read page 29 in 'The Mysteries Box' instruction book.
3 What is the first thing that makes Mr Hawes-Brown think the bottle find 'is interesting'?
4 How do we know that Keith has not turned to his parents for advice?
5 'Witz' is a German word. Try and find out what it means.

C

Write down what you think each of the following words means. Check with a dictionary to see if your definitions are correct.

thoroughly **singe** **antique** **sealed**
representative **examine** **forbids**

D

Re-write the following paragraph. Fill in the blanks with

what you think are suitable words. Check with the 'facts' when you need to.

> We know that Jock has been unable to walk and it seems likely that it was his____ that were injured. Judging by the date of Jock's letter the bottles he is bringing for Alf would seem to be a ____ present. It seems certain that Keith knows his ____ collects ____ bottles. Judging by the evidence of this file it also seems likely that Keith ____ one of his father's bottles.

E

Choose one of the following and with a friend, or friends, prepare either a short mime or play about it.

1 Act out what happens when Mr Hawes-Brown and a committee of important people call in an expert for his opinion of the 'message'.
2 Act out the scene in which Alf Noble finally gets involved in all this.
3 You are a newspaper reporter who follows this whole story through. Act out the scene when you finally tell the editor all that has happened.

F

1 Finish in your own words either, the report in the *Bleeston Argus*, or, the letter to Uncle Fred.
2 Look again at the evidence given and then decide exactly what it was that Keith did. Then say in what order he did these things.
3 Imagine Keith and a friend hide near Bleeston Beach to see if someone picks up the bottle. Write down the conversation they might have had as events took their course.
4 Using a tape recorder, tape how each of the following might have told this story a few weeks afterwards, when all the facts were known: Keith, Mrs Noble, Uncle Fred, Mr Hawes-Brown.